SOUTH AFRICA AND WORLD OPINION

SOUTH AFRICA
AND
WORLD OPINION

by
PETER CALVOCORESSI

Issued under the auspices of the
Institute of Race Relations

OXFORD UNIVERSITY PRESS

LONDON   NEW YORK   TORONTO

1961

Oxford University Press, Amen House, London E.C.4

GLASGOW NEW YORK TORONTO MELBOURNE WELLINGTON
BOMBAY CALCUTTA MADRAS KARACHI KUALA LUMPUR
CAPE TOWN IBADAN NAIROBI ACCRA

Printed in Great Britain

CONTENTS

SOUTH AFRICA AND WORLD OPINION   1–43

APPENDIXES

I

ON 21 March 1960 a crowd of Africans converged on the police station at Sharpeville near Vereeniging in the Transvaal. Other crowds were collecting round other police stations in South Africa on the same day, which had been designated a day of protest against the pass laws. Mr. Robert Sobukwe, President of the Pan-Africanist Congress, had asked the members of his organisation to leave their reference books[1] at home and to go to police stations and court arrest for this breach of the law. They were told to conduct themselves quietly and to eschew violence.

There is not even proximate agreement about the size of the crowd at Sharpeville or its intentions or its actions. Official statements put the number of demonstrators at 15,000 or 20,000 and alleged that they carried firearms and other weapons and attacked the small force of 75 policemen who were on duty. Immediately after the events that followed, the authorities announced that the first shots had come from the crowd and denied that any order to fire had at any time been given to the police. This version was scouted by witnesses, including European witnesses, who estimated the size of the crowd at 3–4,000 and described it as good-natured, cheerful and unarmed. The police, it was said, had fired first, drawn up in a line and firing no warning volley. Most of the resulting victims' wounds were in the back and must have been received as the leading part of the crowd turned to flee.

There was a similar scene at Langa in Cape Province. Altogether that day 72 Africans were reported killed and 180 wounded. The government at once promised judicial

---

[1] These are wallets containing the dozen or so documents which every black male South African over 16 years of age is legally required to have about him. African women of the same age also carry them, although not required by law to do so before 1 December 1960.

enquiries into these happenings and two judges were appointed to investigate and report. Meanwhile Sharpeville had become a household word in five continents.

This booklet is not primarily concerned with affairs within the Union of South Africa. It is not my business here to describe or comment upon the policies, practices or mentalities of the Union government or the African Congresses. I am concerned to show how a single incident, which happened to occur at Sharpeville on 21 March 1960, caught the attention of the world, and what were the consequences of this suddenly increased awareness of a state of affairs which could produce bloodshed and death on this scale in the Union.

There were widespread horror and indignation. Since the advent of the popular press and the radio it has become easier to estimate the extent of the impact of an event on the public mind, although it remains very hard to gauge the depth of the impact or its lastingness. Sharpeville was front-page news all over the world; it was extensively reported and discussed on radio programmes; and in the richer countries of the world the grisly story was further propagated by television. It was therefore brought to an enormously wider audience than, say, the Bulgarian atrocities or Jalianwala Bagh, and in a much more vivid way. It so happened that a reporter, using the resourcefulness which is the stock-in-trade of the journalist's profession, was able to get—and to get away with—some photographs of the Sharpeville affray. The chance availability of this dramatic record may have persuaded editors here and there to give the accompanying news story a prominent place on their front pages, and these pictures were seen by millions.

Nor did the news dry up after the first flush. Incidents continued. So did the campaign against the pass laws. Chief Albert Luthuli, President of the African National Congress, burnt his pass and his example was followed by many others after an announcement that the pass laws were suspended.[2] The Bishop of Johannesburg fled the country and so did many others. Africans stayed away from work in very large numbers. A state of emergency was declared and army and militia units were called up. On the same day, 30 March, 30,000 Africans staged an extraordinary demonstration, marching peaceably and in good order into the centre of Cape Town and back again.[3] In the following weeks thousands of Africans were arrested and kept in prison; four months later it was revealed that 8,600 'idlers' were still so held, besides 1,900 political detainees. The authorities, faced for the first time with a protest that was nation-wide, resorted to the most direct and crude forms of physical violence in their attempts to get African workers back to work. On 9 April a white farmer tried to kill Dr. Verwoerd and only narrowly failed. All these things provided continuing copy for the press and kept the first sharp impact alive. Stories about the use by the police of whips, clubs and guns to force Africans to return to work were specially instrumental in maintaining revulsion against the Union government's doings, and South African papers themselves noted that even the Union's normal defenders in the British and American press had joined in the almost universal denunciation.

Foreign reactions were far from being confined to anti-*apartheid* zealots; even governments and other official bodies joined in the outcry of condemnation. In Norway flags were flown at half-mast on public buildings on the day of the funeral of the Sharpeville victims. At the other side of the world and at rather a different level the Brazilian government banned a football match in Rio de Janeiro against a South African team; it also recalled its ambassador from Pretoria. At a conference in New Zealand the Prime Minister, Mr. Walter Nash, asked his audience to stand in silent memory of the dead and the Indian House of

[2] This announcement was reversed a week later.
[3] This feat was organised by a student of 21, Mr. Patrick Kgosane. He was arrested the next day.

Representatives also paid this tribute before Mr. Nehru moved
a resolution in a speech in which he likened the Nationalists
to the Nazis. Other Commonwealth Prime Ministers,
especially in Asia and Africa, made trenchant comments,
and only Mr. Menzies in Australia took the formally correct
line that what happened in South Africa was the domestic
concern of that country, though even he felt compelled to
instruct the Australian High Commissioner in Pretoria
to make a special enquiry into the facts, causes and significance of the shootings. In Canada Mr. Diefenbaker, speaking in Parliament, deplored the loss of life and said that his
government had no sympathy with policies of racial
discrimination. The House of Commons at Westminster
unanimously adopted a similar resolution, as did various
other parliamentary bodies in different parts of the world.
The action of the Dutch Parliament attracted special
attention because of the links of kinship between the
Netherlands and the Afrikaners. At The Hague the Prime
Minister opened a debate in a packed upper chamber and
the house adopted a resolution calling on the South African
government to look to the welfare of all the inhabitants
of the Union and to give effect to human rights. In the
United States of America the Secretary of State took the
very unusual step of issuing a statement which was as
startling an interference in the affairs of another country
as Lord John Russell's celebrated despatch on Piedmont
nearly one hundred years earlier.

These were the overt acts and expressions. It is difficult
and dangerous to generalise about them but, subject to all
the obvious reservations, it seems worth venturing certain
general comments about the underlying moods evoked and
revealed by the stories which were reaching all parts of the
world from South Africa in the days and weeks after
Sharpeville. First, as regards Europe. Here (though not
exclusively here) the basic sentiment was outraged humanitarianism. What struck home was the sight of death. This
by itself caused horror and disgust among thousands of

people who had no political thoughts in their heads whatever. Comparisons with the Nazis were common. It was also possible to detect a certain feeling of shame, a feeling that here was an evil of which one had been dimly aware for some time but which one had somehow contrived to dodge—even as so many people had managed to turn a blurred eye to Germany's crimes against the Jews in the thirties and preferred not to know too much about the way the French army was even then behaving in Algeria. Europeans had special, if unacknowledged, reasons for dodging the South African issue: it raised the colour problem, about which the European conscience as a whole and the colonial Powers in particular were touchy; it intruded a jarring note into a society which had been trying with some success, in places with considerable success, to get back to an easefulness which had once been Europe's prerogative and was now become part of its dream; and it offended against the civilised European's unwillingness to believe that anything can be wholly bad or utterly beyond repair. Sharpeville shook deeply-seated inherited attitudes.

With Asians it was otherwise. Humanitarianism probably played a lesser part than in Europe, for life in Asia is cheaper and the loss of life, including violent loss of life, no rare thing. While Europeans clung to the notion that two world wars and concentration camps were eccentric interruptions to their way of life, Asians were wont to accept such curses as part of the natural order. Moreover, to Asians Sharpeville was no revelation, for Asia had already consciously judged the Union government to be wicked. Sharpeville was confirmation and Asians could not but feel a certain gratification at the sight of the rest of the world being forced round to their point of view. The colour question too necessarily played a different part in Asian opinion. A significant and distressing factor in the Asian reaction was the rush of latent anti-white feeling to the surface. Indignation against the Nationalist régime in South Africa was much stronger and more widespread than indignation against President Syngman Rhee's mode of government in South Korea, and this distinction was illogical except upon the basis that the offences of a white man call up something which the similar offences of a fellow Asian do not awaken. Allied with this anti-white feeling, but more positive and more conscious, was the feeling of solidarity between Asians and Africans which had its roots in the colonial past and had shown its head above ground at the Bandung conference of 1955. Westerners were apt to belittle this solidarity and they may have been right in regarding it as little more than an 'anti' feeling, effective only when Asians and Africans could make common cause against a shared bogey. But the Union government, being a white minority government in a black continent, was the ideal bogey. At a more practical level Asians had become used to reading a great deal about Africa in the Asian vernacular press in the past five years, so that their minds and their instincts were more alert to what was happening in Africa than had been the case only a short time before.

To generalise about the United States is both more easy and more difficult than to generalise about other large areas. It is easier because the Americans are the most articulate people in the world but against this is their comparative remoteness hitherto from African affairs, a remoteness which deprives the observer (and the Americans themselves) of a background against which to test and judge. Nevertheless it is safe to say that the impact of Sharpeville in the United States was very great indeed. A dozen or more radio stations provided regular commentaries on events in the Union and from coast to coast the press coverage was considerable. As in Europe the first shock was to humanitarian feelings and the second to complacency: what had been vaguely appreciated was made brutally real. The peculiar element in the American reaction was the American Union's own racial problem which had itself, to the shame of countless Americans, become world news at the time of the closing of the schools in Little Rock. Americans needed therefore to differentiate their own problem from that of South Africa. This they were able to do by recalling that the trend in the United States was towards better things while the example of the Nationalists in South Africa pointed in the opposite direction; American law prescribed equality of treatment while South African law imposed discrimination.[4] There was in other words a big moral difference and they could vent righteous indignation against a government which, although confronted with a similar problem, was trying to wrestle with it by eroding instead of bolstering decency, justice and human rights. Finally, it so happened that the impact of Sharpeville coincided with a sharply mounting wave of American interest in African affairs and with growing pressure, public and private, on the administration to make clear its disapproval of the policy of *apartheid*. Americans, though still curiously regarded by Europeans as isolationist and introspective, had become aware of Africa as a continent where important things were happening very fast, a continent into which the contest between the United States and the U.S.S.R. was seeping, a continent about which Americans ought to have knowledge, ideas and policies. African studies were gaining prestige and volume in universities and talks on Africa were in demand in the countless societies up and down the country where seriously-minded citizens gathered for self-improvement. Business circles too were directly concerned. American investment in Africa, although much smaller than British investment, was growing (the banks, for instance, were moving in) and the greater part of it was in the Union. Influential semi-private citizens had been discussing African policy with the Secretary of State, Mr. Herter, a short time before Sharpeville and all these trends and activities contributed to the statement issued by the State Department on 22 March. The Department, after deploring

[4] See for example a letter from Miss Rosalyn Tureck in *The Times*, 1 August 1960.

violence and expressing the hope that the African people in the Union would be able to obtain redress for legitimate grievances by peaceful means, drew attention to the fact that the United States did not usually comment on the internal affairs of countries with which it had normal relations, and then went on to regret the tragic loss of life resulting from measures taken against the demonstrators. This censure was, diplomatically speaking, going very far. Yet there were few to condemn the outspokenness and many who wanted something more. Americans for Democratic Action, for example, wrote to the Secretary of State asking for the recall of the American ambassador and a stop to American purchases of South African gold, and a South Africa Emergency Committee began a campaign for the boycott of all South African goods.

But however reactions might vary from one country or one continent to another, they were alike in showing that the course of international politics had been invaded by a moral issue. This course normally pursues a pragmatic way in a complex of conflicting expediencies, but from time to time a moral issue is added to the tangle of world affairs and then the attention and the imagination of millions of non-political people are caught and even governments will deviate from settled policies or act against their interests (the suppression of the slave trade was a case in point). Sharpeville was an event of this kind. Indignation was not enough. But if the case cried for action, who might act and how, and with what effect?

II

THE Union of South Africa is a member of two international- al organisations, the Commonwealth and the United Nations, and it has valuable bilateral commercial dealings with a number of states. It may therefore be influenced by either of the bodies to which it belongs and it can be damaged by the use of economic weapons. I shall deal first with the Commonwealth connexion.

The Sharpeville affair happened to fall shortly before a Commonwealth Prime Ministers' conference in London, but before considering what happened at that conference it is necessary to go back to the beginning of the year and say something about the very significant visit of the British Prime Minister, Mr. Harold Macmillan, to Africa, which culminated in his famous 'wind of change' speech delivered on 3 February to the South African Parliament in Cape Town.

Mr. Macmillan had made an extensive Commonwealth tour in the winter of 1957/8, visiting on that occasion the Asian and Australasian dominions. He had earlier coupled a visit to Canada with his rendezvous with President Eisenhower in Bermuda immediately after he succeeded Sir Anthony Eden as Prime Minister in 1957. During 1958 and 1959 he was much preoccupied with defence and foreign affairs and the latter year saw his visit to Moscow and other capitals in an attempt to promote a Russo-American *rapprochement* and a summit conference. During these years Africa meant, to Whitehall and the British public, chiefly Kenya and the Central African Federation (especially Nyasaland), where events proceeded in the manner of the legendary snail which climbs painfully up a slippery pole by day only to fall back again before the next day. Elsewhere in Africa Ghana had become an independent dominion, Nigeria was about to follow suit with Tanganyika not far behind, and the French and Belgian territories were skipping political adolescence in a rush from tutelage to full responsibility. At some point in 1959 the British Prime Minister, turning now his attention to Africa, decided to change his policy (with his Colonial Secretary), to push British territories into independence instead of applying a half-hearted brake, and so to make a bid for the friendship of the African nationalisms which

were becoming a force to be reckoned with in world affairs.
He also decided to visit Africa himself, taking in the new
dominion of Ghana, the budding dominion of Nigeria,
the semi-dominion of Southern Rhodesia—and the Union
of South Africa.

There were immediate protests against the last item on
the itinerary. The general public probably did not care
one way or the other as yet, but there were a number
of people specially concerned with African affairs who
feared and said that a visit by the British Prime Minister
to the Union was tantamount to endorsement of the
discriminating legislation and social injustices which had
increasingly marked the régime of the Nationalist Party
since its attainment of power in 1948. On the other hand
to omit the Union would have been a decided affront,
for the Union was by far the oldest of Britain's free African
associates in the Commonwealth and would, if omitted,
have been the only dominion not visited by Mr. Macmillan
since becoming Prime Minister. Moreover Mr. Macmillan
knew what very few people knew at this time. He knew
before he left England for his tour what he was going to say
when he got to Cape Town.

The 'wind of change' speech (delivered six weeks before
Sharpeville) does not make very remarkable reading to a
European casting an eye over it in a European newspaper.
Indeed from a British point of view Mr. Macmillan could
hardly have said less and would certainly have been attacked
by some Conservatives as well as by the Left if he had done
so. He made in effect two points: that things in Africa were
changing and that the British did not like racial discrimination. Both these things were well known and could not have
caused a ripple in the Albert Hall, but when the British
Prime Minister pronounced them in Cape Town the
effect was terrific; the South African Prime Minister was
visibly dumbfounded and as Mr. Macmillan's words
spread beyond the Parliament building Africans received
them with a jubilation that was all the greater because it

sprang from surprise. The speech was a shock, even to those who saw but dimly and could not have formulated its central point: that in future Britain, if forced to a choice between kith and kin and new states in Africa, would choose the latter and that therefore the white minorities in the Union (and in Southern Rhodesia) could not look to a mother country or a big white brother to succour them in their times of trouble. An illusion was shattered. In Britain the most important result of the speech was that thenceforward South African news ranked for more, and more prominent, space in newspapers.

But Mr. Macmillan's political manoeuvres in Africa involved him in difficulties which became apparent at the time of Sharpeville and during the Commonwealth conference. The British Prime Minister was supposed to be a 'Commonwealth man'.[1] He wanted, it appeared, to denounce *apartheid* and at the same time to keep the Commonwealth together. This was, however, no easy task, for Sharpeville brought considerable reinforcement to those who had for some time been saying that the Commonwealth would be better without South Africa. After Sharpeville Mr. Macmillan expressed his 'deep regret' over what had happened but nothing like the State Department's statement issued from the Foreign Office or Downing Street. Britain abstained from voting in the Security Council on 1 April, and the resolution passed by the House of Commons on 8 April, nearly three weeks after Sharpeville, was rather tame.

By adopting policies which led to the Sharpeville affair just before a Commonwealth conference the Union government had undesignedly added a new item to the conference's agenda which was to overshadow all the other items put together. This was no less than the nature of the Commonwealth. Before 1947 the principal links between the

---

[1] The evidence for this is sketchy and the idea may have got around from a comparison of Mr. Macmillan with his predecessor who was notoriously not a Commonwealth man.

dominions were allegiance to the British Crown, kinship, defence obligations and exchanges of information on a scale not practised between other sovereign states even when allied. By 1947, when India, Pakistan and Ceylon became sovereign members of the Commonwealth and Burma left it,[2] all these links were attenuated: republics were accepted as members, people of non-British stock far outnumbered those of British origin, the defence of the Asian and Australasian dominions was no longer secured by British arms and ships, and the exchange of intimate information was necessarily lessened by the widening of the circle, by the fact that dominions were allowed to pursue fundamentally differing foreign policies (India set the example) and by Britain's possession of certain types of technical military information which it was prepared to share with none except the United States, Canada and perhaps Australia. The unity of the Commonwealth was therefore stripped to bedrock and it became apparent that among the whole body of members, old and new, there was one and only one common characteristic. All had at one time or another been subject to the British Crown. The Commonwealth was an association of states linked by their historical fortunes.

The inclination to eject South Africa was, when rationalised, an attempt to say that this qualification for membership was not enough. In addition each member must behave in a certain way. Even if it was difficult to draw the line, there would be cases where clearly the line had been crossed. This new criterion could hardly be cast in democratic postulates since there were quite a number of places in the Commonwealth where democracy did not flourish, but it could be and was urged that there was no room in the Commonwealth for a state which adopted racial discrimination or, more broadly, failed to honour basic

[2] Burma actually left at the beginning of 1948, the change in status being postponed on astrological advice.

human rights. In other words the Commonwealth must be an ideological as well as an historical community. The objections to this concept were various. In the first place the new Commonwealth, with a history of only thirteen years, might not be able to survive the novel shock of an eviction. Secondly, to accept the principle of eviction opened up a prospect of frequent complaints by one member against another, so that the Commonwealth might become a centre of recrimination instead of an exemplar and a tontine. And thirdly, there were those who denounced as priggish the amputation of a whole community on the score that its government was not clubbable.[3]

Before the Prime Ministers assembled in London the attempt on Dr. Verwoerd's life had been made and his place was taken by Mr. Eric Louw, the Union's Minister for External Affairs, a disappointed man who had missed the Premiership and had had his natural rigidity and stubbornness affirmed by the prospect of a future that had no more to offer him. Besides defending his government against the attacks which were bound to come, Mr. Louw's main task was to secure the conference's agreement to South Africa remaining a member of the Commonwealth if and when it decided to become a republic. A referendum on this issue (one of the main planks in the Nationalist programme) was planned and since there were already several republican dominions no trouble had been expected from the conference. On their side the rest of the Commonwealth in conference had two ways of putting pressure on the Union: by expressing massive and unanimous disapproval of *apartheid* and by hedging over the acceptance of the Union as a republican member of the Commonwealth.

[3] The common analogy of the Commonwealth with a club is a mischievous one. In a club a member represents only himself. He may leave or secure the departure of another individual. But the members of the Commonwealth are societies and to evict a society is to stigmatise and perhaps penalise a great number of people who are sinned against and not sinning.

The conference used both these weapons, and among its members there were two distinct motives at work. On the one hand some Prime Ministers, for example the Malayan, were under an obligation or compulsion to protest as powerfully and formally as possible; for the rest, there was an optimistic feeling, which in retrospect looks very odd, that the South African leaders could be prevailed upon to change their policies. The turning-point in the conference was the realisation by his colleagues of Mr. Louw's embattled intransigence.

The question of *apartheid* was not placed on the conference's formal agenda. In order to avoid a complete breakdown Mr. Macmillan exerted himself to secure a compromise whereby *apartheid* would only be discussed informally at a series of meetings which Mr. Louw would have with his various colleagues. Mr. Macmillan was supported by Mr. Nehru and other Prime Ministers who disliked the idea of expulsion since it impinged on the principle of domestic sovereignty. When the conference opened on 3 May the Malayan Prime Minister, Tungku Abdul Rahman, proposed that *apartheid* be included in the agenda, a course to which he had pledged himself before leaving Malaya, but when Mr. Louw objected on the grounds that the matter was South Africa's private and domestic concern, Mr. Macmillan's compromise was adopted and for a time the thorny subject was tucked away. Mr. Louw did not object to private talks and appeared to believe that he would be explaining to the other Prime Ministers things which they did not understand and would be able to convert them, or some of them, from a prejudiced hostility towards his government. But on 4 May Mr. Louw gave a press conference which so infuriated many of the other Prime Ministers that on the following day the Tungku walked out of a meeting at No. 10 Downing Street, refused to continue the informal talks and issued a statement in which he demanded action against South Africa and hinted at an international boycott. Mr. Macmillan contrived to fend off disaster and a few days later the informal discussions were resumed with all Prime Ministers present, though on the same day Dr. Nkrumah cancelled an invitation to Mr. Louw to visit Ghana. The conference came to an end on 13 May with a communiqué[4] which said very little about *apartheid*, but by that time Mr. Louw could be in no doubt that the whole Commonwealth was resolutely opposed to South African policies and that some members were determined to do more than protest. Both at the informal sessions and at public meetings before or after the conference various Prime Ministers, white as well as non-white, had used strong words to describe what was going on in the Union.

Mr. Louw failed too to get what he wanted on the continued membership of South Africa if it became a republic. Approval was given to the admission of a Ghanaian republic but the conference was able to distinguish the Ghanaian from the South African case because in Ghana a referendum on the form of the state had already been held, whereas in South Africa it was still to come (and would be conducted only among a minority of the population). Consequently the South African application was held over and the communiqué gave a hint that if the application were renewed before the Union's racial policies had been changed, it might be rejected. Mr. Louw signed the communiqué which contained this threat after consulting Dr. Verwoerd by telephone.

So the conference succeeded in preventing the South African issue from disrupting its deliberations and contrived a formula to express disapproval without provocation. Yet when the week's work was done, there was a flavour of failure in the air. The forum and the timing were the best available for administering a rebuke to the Union government. The other governments had shown how they felt but had apparently cleared their consciences by

[4] See below p. 56

unburdening their minds. Mr. Macmillan's endeavours to avoid ructions and rifts at the conference had prevented the senior member of the Commonwealth from giving a lead on the issue of substance, and the desire to stick together had overridden the impulse to make the Commonwealth an example of good government and decent behaviour. As a result there was some foreboding that the Commonwealth had dug its own grave. Although a difficult passage had been negotiated by skilful political conjuring, the vital problem of how to maintain an association which had been invaded by hatred had not been solved. It had been postponed but postponed, one felt, merely because postponement was the least obnoxious outcome to the greatest number of the associates. It was hard to detect any belief that by postponement the problem could be made to disappear or a genuine solution would turn up. Perhaps some of the Commonwealth leaders were hoping against hope for changes in South African politics so significant as to relax the tension and induce the Union's Commonwealth partners to give it another chance. Perhaps on the other hand other leaders were hoping that the Union would itself force the issue by becoming a republic and so lay itself open to a refusal to endorse its continued membership of the Commonwealth. The latter seemed the more likely, if the less attractive, course[5] but if either materialised the delaying tactics of the London conference would have been vain, the problem would recur, meanwhile some members of the Commonwealth were bound to seek for ways outside the Commonwealth to put an end to minority and discriminatory rule in the Union, and these attempts would themselves create intolerable strains within the Commonwealth.

[5] At the beginning of August Dr. Verwoerd announced that a referendum on the form of the state would be held on 5 October. There was some suggestion that if thereafter he could negotiate with Great Britain a relationship similar to that of Britain with Eire, he would accept exclusion from the Commonwealth with equanimity.

III

THE second forum in which South Africa could be attacked was the United Nations. In the case of the Commonwealth the principal threat had been the implied refusal to renew membership if and when renewal became necessary, and the Union was placed in the position of either changing its policies or postponing the referendum on the republic if it wished to be sure of remaining in the Commonwealth. In the case of the United Nations there was never any question of expulsion and the first moves in the Security Council had an air of unreality, but a possible weapon lay to hand in South Africa's position as the mandatory Power in relation to South West Africa.

On 23 March the African delegates to the United Nations held a meeting in New York and the next day they asked for an immediate meeting of the Security Council to consider the events in the Union on the basis that they constituted a threat to peace and security. This move was immediately backed by the State Department and when the Council met, the United States delegate, Mr. Cabot Lodge, argued that the proceedings were not a contravention of Article 2 (7) of the Charter (which lays down that the United Nations may not interfere in matters which are essentially within the domestic jurisdiction of a state) and that Article 2 (7) should be read in conjunction with Articles 55 and 56 (which engage all members to promote economic betterment, social progress and fundamental freedoms).[1] The South African delegate, Mr. Bernardus Fourie, naturally argued strongly to the contrary but without success, the Council taking the view that Article 2 (7) did not apply to the inscription and discussion of an agenda item. In the ensuing debate the British Foreign Secretary, Mr. Selwyn Lloyd, supported his South African colleague on the question of jurisdiction and maintained that

---

[1] See p. 57 below for the text of Articles 2 (7), 55 and 56.

Article 2 (7) prevailed over Articles 55 and 56; the French member took the same line. On 1 April the Council approved by nine votes to nil with two abstentions (Britain and France) a resolution proposed by Ecuador which declared that the situation in South Africa had led to international friction and might, if continued, endanger international peace and security; deplored the loss of life at Sharpeville and Langa and extended sympathy to the families of the victims; deplored the policies of the South African government and called upon it to take measures aimed at racial harmony and to abandon *apartheid* and racial discrimination; and charged the Secretary-General of the United Nations, in consultation with the South African government, to make arrangements whereby the purposes and principles of the Charter would be upheld.

Mr. Hammarskjöld was now in a difficulty since he was required to do something which he had no means of effecting. Though he might consult with the South African government (if the South African government were willing to consult with him), he seemed to have no prospect whatever of getting it to change its policies and his role seemed therefore to be limited to making a *démarche* and then reporting back to the Security Council that he had failed to achieve anything. In this way the Council would remain seised of the matter but nothing else would happen. However, Mr. Hammarskjöld was able on 19 April to report that he would be going to London to talk to South African Ministers at the conclusion of the Commonwealth conference, preparatory to going to South Africa itself at the end of July or early in August. This was more than most people had expected and was reckoned a success for Mr. Hammarskjöld.

Meanwhile a new gambit presented itself. South Africa administered or, as its critics maintained, maladministered a mandate over South West Africa. Could this circumstance be used in order to bring pressure to bear on the Union government? Before examining this question a few words of explanation and history are necessary.

A mandated area is a piece of territory abstracted by conquest from the German or the Ottoman empire at the end of the First World War and allotted to one or another of the victorious Powers by the Supreme Council of the Allied and Associated Powers in accordance with Article 22 of the Covenant of the League of Nations[2] and the relevant Peace Treaty. Such areas were lost to the German or Ottoman empire but were not gained by the mandatory Power, the mandate being an invention designed to take territory away from A without giving it to B. The mandatory had no power to annex the territory in question but held it, as the name implied, in trust and subject to certain supervisory functions vested in the Council of the League and the Permanent Mandates Commission. The League's powers were likewise limited, for although it had supervisory rights and machinery, it was not clear how, if at all, it could redress any misdemeanours disclosed by the supervisors.

The question whether a mandate may be revoked has never been decided; nor has it ever come formally before a competent tribunal. There was much discussion during the twenties and thirties concerning the termination of a mandate. Was a mandate temporary or permanent in character? Did the termination of a mandate depend only upon the fulfilment of certain conditions concerning the capacity of the mandated territory (and if so, was this fulfilment a question of fact?) or was it also proper for and incumbent upon the League to exact guarantees about the future? Was the consent of the mandatory a further precondition to the termination of a mandate? These questions were raised, first in the twenties because the prospects of securing private investment in a mandated territory seemed the poorer if the mandate were to be regarded as a fleeting arrangement, and secondly at the

[2] See below, p. 59, for the text of this article.

time when Great Britain proposed to promote Iraq from mandated to independent status. Neither the Council of the League nor the Permanent Mandates Commission nor a special sub-committee established by the latter to consider these matters was confronted with the problem of terminating a mandate by forfeiture against the will of the mandatory, but the discussions produced certain *obiter dicta* with a bearing on this more thorny issue. Lord Lugard, for instance, in a report calculated to reassure private investors, supposed that revocation could for all practical purposes be regarded as inconceivable, but he went on to envisage it in a case of gross violation of the mandate agreement and at the instance of the International Court. The Permanent Mandates Commission, in recommendations subsequently adopted by the Council, assumed that the 'cessation or transfer' of a mandate was possible, though the Commission was not then concerned to examine the prerequisite circumstances and conditions (except in a special sense not here relevant). One report presented to the Commission expressly referred to the possibility of the forfeiture of a mandate but this view would seem to conflict with another to the effect that a mandate, being a bilateral contract, could not be abrogated without the consent of the mandatory. Revocation remains therefore a legal conundrum.[3] If a mandate can neither be enforced nor revoked, then a mandatory is in a position of trust but cannot be made to fulfil this trust. This is a position abhorred by equity but not unknown in practice nor unknown to the law.

Even if a mandatory can be called to book, there remains the question who has the right to sit in judgment upon him and, in the extreme case, revoke the mandate. The judicial function could properly be assumed by the International Court but the Court has no executive competence. Since

[3] For a more detailed and scholarly discussion of these matters see 'The General Principles Governing the Termination of a Mandate', by Luther Harris Evans, in *The American Journal of International Law*, vol. 26, 1932, pp. 735 ff.

the mandates were not given by the League but by the Supreme Council, it would seem doubtful, to say the least, whether the League or (now) the United Nations could take away what it neither gave nor ever had in its gift. It can, however, be argued that even if the United Nations do not have this power, the original donors, i.e. the Supreme Council, have. The Supreme Council consisted of Britain, France, Italy, Japan and the United States of America. After the Second World War Italy and Japan abandoned their rights under the Treaty of Versailles and the powers of the Supreme Council (if any) are accordingly now vested in the British, French and American governments, who may conceivably have certain rights in this respect, though they would clearly be reluctant to assert them (Great Britain particularly so because of the Commonwealth considerations already referred to).

South West Africa, formerly known as German South West Africa, was and remains a Class C mandate.[4] The administration of this mandate was entrusted in December 1920 to King George V in right of his sovereignty over the Union of South Africa, which means, constitutional formalities apart, that the Union administers the territory which has an area of rather more than 300,000 square miles. The Union was authorised to govern South West Africa as an integral part of the Union. Upon the dissolution of the League of Nations its surviving functions descended to the United Nations. A government which had been entrusted with a mandate by the Supreme Council was under no obligation to transform the mandated area into a trusteeship territory as defined and invented by the Charter of the United Nations, but equally it was not relieved of its obligations under the mandate. The other mandated territories in Africa—Tanganyika, Ruanda-Urundi and the Cameroons—were converted into trusteeship territories

[4] For classes of mandate see Article 22 of the Covenant of the League, below, p. 59. A class C mandate is a mandate still fully within sub-clause 6 of this Article.

by agreements between the British, Belgian and French governments respectively and the United Nations, but the South African government preferred not to take this step and the International Court of Justice confirmed its right to ignore the repeated requests of the United Nations to negotiate a trusteeship agreement. But the South African government's disdain of the United Nations went further than that. It not only refused to place the territory under trusteeship but also neglected to deliver the annual report required by the mandate agreement[5] and to forward petitions presented to it by the inhabitants for transmission to the Committee on South West Africa which the United Nations set up to discharge the continuing functions of the Permanent Mandates Commission. This Committee, which was asked by the General Assembly in February 1957 to enquire what legal action could be taken, by the United Nations or members of the United Nations or former members of the League individually or jointly, to ensure the performance of the mandate, duly presented a report which recited the rulings of the International Court on the legal position and reported that the policy of *apartheid* was a 'flagrant violation of the sacred trust which permeated the mandate'. This report was approved by the General Assembly in November 1959 and by the time of Sharpeville four months later people were still wondering what, if anything, could be done either to make the South African government mend its ways or to take the mandate away from it. Alleged infractions of the mandate agreement included failure to promote the material and moral well-being of the inhabitants of the territory, failure to suppress the slave trade and forced labour, failure to observe the ban on the construction of naval and military bases and fortifications, failure to ensure freedom of conscience and religion, and failure to permit freedom of movement for missionaries.

At the Commonwealth conference in May Dr. Nkrumah

[5] See below, p. 61, for the text of this agreement.

raised informally the question of asking South Africa to surrender the mandate (a precedent for surrender existed in the case of Palestine where the mandate had been voluntarily returned to the United Nations by the mandatory) but nothing was done owing to the fear that South Africa would leave the Commonwealth if confronted with such a request. The British government was particularly unwilling to have the question treated as a Commonwealth matter because of the obviously disruptive implications of this course and Commonwealth action was ruled out so long as any appreciable number of members gave pride of place to keeping the Commonwealth together. Some members, however, with Ghana in the lead, had a different order of priorities and seemed prepared to force the pace on South West Africa even if the existence of the Commonwealth were jeopardised in the process. Further action was, however, left to non-Commonwealth states. Ethiopia and Liberia, after seeking professional legal advice in the United States, decided to bring the matter once more before the International Court, and in June the conference of independent African states at Addis Ababa[5] was able to place on record the intention of these two countries to institute contentious proceedings regarding South Africa's international obligations in relation to the mandate.

IV

IF persuasion was unavailing and armed force unthinkable, what were the prospects of economic pressure? The idea of besieging a community in peacetime in order to get it to perform or abstain from certain actions was not a new one but the history of similar ventures in the past was not encouraging. It could however be argued that past failures of economic sanctions were to be ascribed more to half-heartedness in applying them than to any inherent weakness

[5] See below, p. 64.

in the weapon itself. In many cases the deficiency lay in the
political will and not in the economic means available. In
any case two things were necessary: first, economic power
which was on balance superior to that of the state to be
compelled, together with a willingness to accept incidental
economic damage in the process of bringing this superior
economic power to bear; and secondly, the readiness, on a
calculation of political expediencies, to break off relations
with the intended victim. And these two things had to be
present in the same breast, for if the states capable of doing
economic damage were not the states willing to break off
relations, then the outcast whom it was sought to humble
had little to fear.

The South African economy was strong, getting stronger
but far from self-sufficient. The post-war years were boom
years in which the mining and export of gold, uranium and
diamonds expanded rapidly[1] and produced a comple-
mentary development of the road and rail facilities needed
to move these precious products from mine to port of
embarkation. Agriculture, the twin prop of the South
African economy, also expanded and the Union became
self-sufficient in wheat and an important exporter of wool.
Alongside these two established sectors new industrial
activities were growing up and manufactured goods helped
to keep the balance of payments healthy; in 1959 the Union
exported steel.

This all-round expansion could not have been effected
without a substantial injection of foreign capital, nor had
the Union's industrial evolution reached the stage where it
could itself provide the fresh capital required to maintain
the pace of development. During the eight years 1950–7
foreign funds contributed 10 per cent to the formation of
new capital in the Union and had provided that essential
external stimulus without which domestic capital formation

[1] In 1959 the value of mined gold and uranium was £250 million and
£49 million respectively. The total mining output was, at £385 million,
a record. See the speech of Sir Edmund Hall-Patch at the annual general
meeting of the Standard Bank of South Africa on 27 July 1960.

can hardly get under way. In the decade ending on 31 March 1958 South Africa multiplied its external debt by six.[2] Loans were raised publicly in London, New York, Amsterdam and Zürich and further credits obtained from the International Bank, the International Monetary Fund and the Export Import Bank.[3] Even more important was private investment which averaged £70 million a year from 1948 to 1954. This trend was reversed after 1954 and in 1957 there was a net capital loss of £29 million, but in the following year there was again a net gain of £55 million.[4] More than half of all foreign investment took the form of investment in companies controlled outside South Africa ('direct investment'). A very large proportion of foreign money went into the private sector of the South African economy, and in this sector, which at the end of 1956 accounted for 87 per cent of all foreign investment, direct investment was as high as 63 per cent.[5] Britain was the major supplier and something like two-thirds of foreign direct investment, and 40 per cent of foreign indirect investment, came from and was held by individuals or bodies resident in the United Kingdom. The American stake was smaller and was concentrated chiefly in mining. French and Swiss investors followed a long way behind. No other private source was of any practical significance. At the end of 1956, the last date for which precise figures are available, foreign investment amounted to £1,396 million and by the end of 1959 this figure was believed to have grown further to about £1,580 million, half of which or more came from Britain.[6]

South Africa could be attacked economically in three

[2] The total long-term external debt increased by £SA 68·5 million: see *Economic Survey of Africa since 1950*, United Nations, Department of Economic and Social Affairs, New York (1959), p. 226.

[3] For details see ibid., pp. 223, 226, 235, 236.

[4] Ibid., p. 230.

[5] Ibid., p. 230. For details of the distribution of foreign investment, direct and indirect, in the private sector see ibid., p. 238.

[6] *Financial Times*, 31 March 1960. The American stake at this date was estimated at £250 million.

ways: by denying it fresh capital and withdrawing existing capital; by cutting off supplies of essential commodities; and by boycotting South African exports.

Attractive though it was from the economic point of view, South Africa had already before Sharpeville begun to scare investors on political grounds and there had been some movement of capital out of the Union for about two years. Sharpeville greatly accentuated this movement of opinion and funds. Shares in South African companies were at once sold in large quantities and at rapidly falling prices, holders in Paris, Brussels and Zurich leading the way. The declaration of a state of emergency on 30 March was taken as a further alarm signal and on that day alone the aggregate value of the shares dealt in on the Johannesburg stock exchange fell by £70 million, gold shares losing 5 per cent of their market value. By the middle of May the loss since the beginning of the year was more than £600 million. The strike of African workers also affected South African industry and foreign observers. In Cape Town two million man-hours were lost in five days at an estimated cost of £2 million and the total damage caused by the strike was put at £10 million.[7] At the end of May Mr. Harry Oppenheimer told shareholders in the Anglo American Corporation that it would be imprudent to count on raising enough money at reasonable terms from the public, at home or overseas, for new ventures and that four large-scale projects had had to be put into cold storage because the Corporation's overseas associates were unwilling to proceed with them until the political situation in the Union became clearer.

The Union's reserves were in a better state to take the strain of foreign nervousness and disapproval than they would have been a few years earlier. The deficit on overseas trading had been reduced, largely by increased exports of gold which were doubled during the fifties and by restraint on imports which rose by only 50 per cent in the same

[7] *Johannesburg Star*, 23 April 1960.

period. As a result the reserves had reached a peak of
£157.3 million at the end of January 1960 and they stood
at £153.2 million on the eve of Sharpeville. Then the
drain came. The loss in the last week of March amounted
to £7.9 million and in the two months after Sharpeville
the total sank by £34.1 million. With the possibility of
further serious losses a decline to £100 million was envisaged.[8]

Any attempt to injure a country by cutting off supplies
tends to focus in the first place on oil. South Africa's own
output of crude oil is negligible.[9] Practically the whole of
its imports come from the Middle East—86 per cent in
1959 and as much as 93–96 per cent in the preceding three
years.[10] The Union is therefore highly vulnerable to concerted action in the Middle East, the more so since its
stocks at any one time are not thought to exceed 4–6 weeks'
consumption at normal rates. On the other hand such
concerted action as a result of Sharpeville seemed on the
whole unlikely. Governments with no surplus for export,
e.g. the United Arab Republic, might agitate for a boycott[11]
but the producing countries had to weigh more material
considerations. The market in oil had been undergoing
a profound change from seemingly inexhaustible demand to
something like a glut, and therefore any move to starve
South Africa would force the oil companies to cut back
production and so diminish both their own profits and the
royalties which nourished the economies and appetites of

---

[8] The Bank Rate was raised from 4 per cent to 4½ per cent on 10 August,
by which date the reserves were down to £104·3 million.
[9] 48,000 tons in 1957: *Economic Survey of Africa since 1950*, p. 132.
[10] For more detailed figures see below, p. 67. In the years 1955–7
inclusive the Union spent an annual average of $92.3 million on the
import of petroleum and related products. These imports represented
6.5 per cent of total imports: ibid., p. 36.
[11] The U.A.R. had a special interest in boycotts and in spite of the fact
that the closing of the Suez Canal to tankers would have been a breach
of the Convention of Constantinople of 1888, President Nasser might
have been tempted if the active sponsors of the boycott in Africa had
offered at the same time to endorse and extend the Arab boycott of
Israel. But Israel had already and wisely made friends in Africa.

Middle Eastern states and rulers. Moreover, first place among South Africa's suppliers had passed from Saudi Arabia (42 per cent in 1956) to Iran (75 per cent in 1958 and 69 per cent in 1959), and while the former's policy might just conceivably have been affected by an anti-South African pan-Arab movement, the latter's almost certainly could not.

The operation of a boycott does not depend exclusively on the attitudes of those who have been supplying the designated commodity. It is also necessary to take into account other producers who have not been supplying the intended victim but might step in and do so. There was in this case one possible supplier of great importance: the U.S.S.R.

There was no practical reason why the Russians should not send oil to South Africa from the Black Sea, and whatever the views of the South African government about communism there was every reason to suppose that it would prefer Russian oil to no oil. The Russians had an exportable surplus.[12] Tankers were on offer[13] and a siege of the South African economy by Middle Eastern oil interests could probably be broken by the Russians in about four weeks. For this reason such a siege seemed improbable, even if the other obstacles just mentioned were to be ignored or overcome. In economic terms the Middle Eastern producers and royalty owners were nervous of letting the Russians into a part of their traditional market in a time of surplus, and in political terms the Middle East had become increasingly sensitive to Russian initiatives since the Iraqi revolution of 1958 had produced a threat of open or creeping communist dominance in an Arab state. A few years earlier the Arabs would probably have turned a deaf ear to any suggestions that a refusal to supply South Africa would be a golden opportunity for Russian advances, but by

[12] About 24 million tons in 1959, of which 17 million tons went outside the communist block.
[13] Tanker tonnage laid up amounted to some 4 million.

1960 they were thinking of such arguments for themselves.

They may have been unduly apprehensive. From the Russian point of view an offer to supply South Africa was a commercial gambit with a considerable political flaw in it. The Russians had been as keen as anybody to court independent African and Asian states, and Moscow could not go to the help of South Africa without affronting and infuriating the Afro-Asian block; communist comments on Sharpeville were as forcefully anti-Afrikaner as any. It is difficult to imagine any circumstances in which this game would have been worth the candle. The Western Powers would certainly have been overjoyed if the U.S.S.R. had committed the blunder of publicly aligning itself with Afrikaner nationalism. Yet the possibility remained, sufficient to give the Arabs pause—or an excuse for abstaining from a course whose moral appeal was offset by substantial material disadvantages.

Oil is an obvious candidate for a selective boycott because of its basic importance in any developed or developing economy and also because its concentration in a relatively few areas of the world and among a small number of major operators facilitates effective joint action. But oil is not the largest of South African imports nor the only commodity through which the South African economy is vulnerable to outside action. Much the biggest group of imports—and one which has been increasing rapidly—comprises metals, metal manufactures, machinery and vehicles.[14] Here the obstacles to a boycott are different, though not less severe.

Far and away South Africa's most important supplier is the United Kingdom, from which the Union draws nearly one-third (in value) of its external needs. The U.S.A. comes second (at 17 per cent in 1959), followed at some distance

[14] Ibid., p. 165. This group accounted for 45.4 per cent of total imports in 1957. Drugs, chemicals and fertilisers, though representing only 4 per cent, have also been increasing, while fibres, yarns, textiles and apparel (17.6 per cent) and food, beverages and tobacco (4.1 per cent) have been proportionately declining.

by Federal Germany, Canada, Japan, the Netherlands and the Central African Federation.[15] Between them these seven states provided South Africa with 71 per cent of its imports in 1959. No single country except Britain and the U.S.A. is in a position seriously to damage the South African economy by cutting off supplies and no combination of countries which excludes these two is likely to get very far. But these were not the countries most eager for action on the economic front.

On the other side of the ledger Britain is almost equally important ranking first in the list of importers from South Africa as it does among South Africa's suppliers. In second place comes the Central African Federation with the United States third and then a quartet of western European countries. Between them these seven countries absorbed 65 per cent of South African exports in 1959,[16] Britain alone taking nearly one-third (exclusive of gold). The pattern of these exports has changed markedly in recent years. The value of exports of gold has more than doubled since before the war in spite of the fact that the price of gold has remained the same. Gold is the largest item and also accounts for a larger proportion of export revenue than any other category. Agricultural exports have risen sharply in value though their proportion of total exports has risen only a little. Two other categories, negligible before the war, have become very important; these are manufactured goods, and minerals and metals.[17] These four categories embrace the whole of South Africa's visible exports and any refusal by its leading customers to continue purchases in any category would be extremely serious. But again any such refusal seems unlikely. The countries which have the power to hurt South Africa are unwilling to use it, while those who wish to do so lack the economic power. Moreover a great part of these exports are by their nature

[15] For details see below, p. 67.
[16] For details see below, p. 67.
[17] For details see below, p. 68.

designed for official or corporate purchasers and not for individuals, who do not buy gold, minerals or metals. Individuals may be prevailed upon to stop buying South African fruit and wine (especially if the banned South African oranges lie in the shops next to morally unexceptionable Australian apples or Israeli grapes) but governments and manufacturers are not so easily prevailed upon to go without uranium, nor is it by any means certain that the individual who abstains from South African fruit for a few weeks would endorse a more serious boycott which would raise the prices of the things he wants to buy or even put him out of work.[18]

Nevertheless Mr. Ben Schoeman, the Union's Minister of Transport, said in June that the Union was facing the most difficult position it had had to face in fifty years and that if the boycott movements which had sprung up in almost every country gained momentum and support the Union would be in a bad way economically. These movements, which began as unofficial protests and developed in some places into government policy, succeeded in imposing complete or considerable boycotts on South African goods in India, the West Indies, the United Arab Republic, Sudan, Malaya and Ghana, while some European countries—notably Norway, Sweden and Denmark—were toying with similar measures. Although South Africa's trade with these countries was not large, the Union government probably feared that the practice would spread, especially if a few striking examples encouraged the boycotters and caught the imagination of the public. One such example occurred early in June when dockers in Trinidad declared they would refuse to unload the s.s. *African Lightning* outward bound from Durban. The dockers were not even willing to fuel and supply the vessel, which had to proceed to New York before returning to

---

[18] The principal effect of the boycott of South African goods in Britain in March was, one may conjecture, to make people think about what was happening in the Union.

Durban with her cargo still on board. This episode received a good deal of publicity and although the West Indian share of South Africa's exports was less than .002 per cent, the gesture of the Trinidad dockers was more baneful than this figure might suggest. Even before Sharpeville, in December 1959, a resolution of the I.C.F.T.U. had called on the 56 million members of the confederation in 100 different countries to boycott South African goods, and this measure had been approved and adopted by the British, West German, Scandinavian and other Trade Union Councils.

African countries, where the will to attack the Union government is strongest, do relatively little trade with the Union. They provide less than 10 per cent of its imports and although they take almost a quarter of its exports, much the greater part of these is bought by the Central African Federation, whose government does not share black Africa's keenness to make the Union government's position as uncomfortable as possible[19]. Nevertheless the conference of independent African states which assembled at Addis Ababa in June addressed itself with vigour and some originality to the problem of damaging the Union's economy. Eleven independent states attended the conference and as many dependent territories sent observers. The conference lasted two weeks and passed a number of resolutions,[20] of which two related to South Africa. The first of these, on South West Africa, has already been

[19] South Africa's imports from African countries in 1950–7 constituted 8.3 per cent of total imports. Exports to African countries account for 22.6 per cent of the total: ibid., p. 152. In the last of these years the total value of South African exports to African countries was $243.7 million, of which $188.8 millions' worth went to the Federation and $54.9 millions' worth to the whole of the rest of Africa. Ghana, Nigeria, Sierra Leone and the territories of French West and Equatorial Africa took between them $6.8 millions' worth: ibid., p. 183.

[20] A report on the conference, giving many of the speeches and all the resolutions, has been published: *Second Conference of Independent African States, Addis Ababa, 14–26 June 1960*, Ministry of Information of the Imperial Ethiopian Government, Addis Ababa (1960).

referred to.[21] The second enumerated a number of ways of bringing pressure to bear on the Union. It invited the African members of the Commonwealth to do all they could to secure the expulsion of the Union from that body. It invited Arab states to approach oil companies with a view to stopping oil from going to South Africa and recommended that no African state should grant any concession to a company which continued to supply the Union. It recommended recourse to Article 41 of the Charter of the United Nations under which the Security Council is empowered, in seeking to give effect to its decisions by means other than armed force, to call on members of the United Nations to impose economic sanctions, to sever diplomatic relations, and to interrupt rail, sea, air, postal, telegraphic and radio communications. Most important of all it called on the members of the conference themselves to take certain steps. These were: to sever or refrain from entering upon diplomatic relations with the Union; to close their ports to vessels flying the South African flag; to prohibit their own ships from entering South African ports; to boycott all South African goods; and to refuse landing and passage facilities to aircraft belonging to the South African government or to any company registered under South African law, and to prohibit such aircraft from using the air space over independent African states. The air boycott was the most striking and novel item in this list but it was not immediately clear whether it was likely to be more effective than the other measures recommended. As if to accentuate the feeling of revulsion which prompted these steps Ghana added in July a provision of its own which, reminiscent of the anti-communist declarations required by the United States immigration laws, exacted from any South African citizen seeking to enter Ghana a formal renunciation of policies of racial discrimination.

[21] See above, p. 23. For the text of the two resolutions affecting South Africa see below, p. 65.

V

THE world felt strongly about Sharpeville but did not know what to do. First emotions were everywhere much the same—horror, indignation, disgust; but when it came to translating emotions into action opinion was less firm and also divided. The world saw a régime that was powerful in a country that was prosperous; serving the interests of a section that was stubbornly convinced that what was being done ought to be done; and inspired by the fierce impulses of a century of unsuccessful nationalism which could not go on being unsuccessful without sacrificing its central purpose as well as the livelihood and even the lives of Afrikaners. The sense of outrage evoked by Sharpeville was therefore accompanied and blunted by a sense of perplexity and even by a sense of helplessness. A speech by a Minister like Mr. Paul Sauer or an industrialist like Mr. Harry Oppenheimer, an initiative like the Commonwealth's expostulation or the attempt to use the South West African mandate as a lever, offered gleams of hope and encouraged the belief that injustice and inhumanity would not after all go unpunished and unchecked, but four months after Sharpeville, when this booklet was being written, the Nationalist government looked as strong and durable as before, while international opinion and international organs seemed to have no more than marginal effects at best. The hard surface might conceal a technical fault destined to become a great crack, but the ear had to strain hard for any sound of disintegration and such sounds as it could catch were of ambiguous import. Dr. Verwoerd's government was constitutionally irremoveable in the sense that it was under no obligation to hold an early election and in little danger of losing one, if held. It was also secure in the further sense that it could maintain itself by the use of force and by virtue of the fact that the Africans could hardly afford to make protracted use of their most effective weapon, the refusal to work. It was sheltered from the sharpest effects of external disapproval because ultimate sovereign power still rested with the state and international action was circumscribed by the rules and habits of an international society which exalted the state above the collectivity of states and also above the individual citizen in the state. Finally, it benefited from its possession of a certain international consequence; besides its valuable and coveted minerals it had a peripheral strategic importance which made the major Western Powers hesitate to alienate it irretrievably or to see it plunged into chaos.

Before going on to consider the courses left open to outsiders by these constricting considerations, it is necessary to say a few words about the last of them—South Africa's strategic contributions to the West in deterring or fighting a major war. These can be shortly enumerated. First, there is the supply of uranium. Secondly, the British navy has the use of the naval base at Simonstown. Thirdly, it is at least convenient to have the right to station military stores and forces in African territories in peacetime, in order that they may be readily despatched to reinforce allies or defend strong-points further east. The Union is in some ways the least convenient African territory for this purpose simply because it is the furthest south, but it is expedient for the strategist to multiply his possibilities and though he might prefer to have his stores and troops further north, he will also like to have elbow-room to the south. What applies to stores and troops applies equally to fly-over and landing rights for aircraft.

These advantages do not stand up to close examination. Stocks of uranium are important but when war comes it does not matter where this uranium was mined or where more of it could be mined. Naval bases and fly-over rights have lost their importance in an age when British strategy is not based on the concept of an island fortress sustained through years of war by keeping communications open to the rest of the world. And finally, having forces and stores handy in Africa is in practice an aspect of particular policies (especially in regard to the Arab sheikhdoms) in which Britain can hardly persevere for much longer in any case. On specialist grounds therefore the strategic arguments for a pact with South Africa are thin and getting thinner.

Strategy includes, however, other non-specialist considerations and on a view of these the balance tilts even more heavily against any close association with a régime such as that of the South African Nationalists. There is, it is true, a sense in which friendship with a white government has seemed more valuable than friendship with a black one; the stability of the black government is often doubtful and it is expected sooner or later to adopt a neutralist foreign policy which would rule out military alliances and the dispensing of military facilities to other states. But there comes a point when friendship with a white government does more harm than good. Africa's importance to the West lies in its attitude in cold war or competitive co-existence in a period when the southern hemisphere is playing an independent part in international power politics for the first time. The defection of chunks of Africa to the communist side would mean the outflanking of western and southern Europe and North America (i.e. the Nato block). In this situation the general goodwill of Africans becomes a cardinal factor in international affairs and the contest for the minds of men overrides such specialist strategic advantages as may be found in alliance with one particular state or another.

This trend in Western thinking was gaining ground in 1960 and it was of course not to the advantage of the South African government. Both Mr. Macmillan and General de Gaulle appeared to have decided to make a strong bid for the friendship of the new or emerging black African states. Mr. Macleod's appointment as Colonial Secretary in place of Mr. Lennox-Boyd was taken as a sign that the British government intended to accelerate the disposal of its colonial responsibilities and tribulations, and Mr. Macmillan's 'wind of change' speech shortly afterwards was a wide advertisement of how top minds were working in London. At the same time General de Gaulle, in an attempt perhaps to retrieve the shocking follies committed by the French in Guinea when it opted out of the French Union, first gave independence in the Union to Mali and Madagascar and then gave independence to the four Entente States (Ivory Coast, Dahomey, Volta, Niger) without even requiring prior settlement of the terms of their membership of the Union. For some years the British and the French had been watching the Germans and the Italians, who were free of the colonial incubus, laying themselves out to make friends and money in Africa, while the Americans, hoping to make up in that continent for a generation's disappointments and mistakes in the Far East, were applying themselves with characteristic thoroughness and generosity to doing good and reaping the promised, if elusive, rewards of virtue. Now the British and French too were hurrying to put themselves right with black Africa— in the French case despite Algeria, in the British case by (among other things) dissociating themselves from racial discrimination in the Union.

In sum, the strategic importance of Africa was considerable but the strategic assets of South Africa were shrinking and were coming to be accounted a lesser prize than the friendship of Africans between the Sahara and the Limpopo. The Western Powers would be reluctant to break with the Union but the Union was not in a position to coerce or blackmail Western governments. In the light of this discussion we revert to the question of what these governments, which above all others had the power to hurt the Union, could do, wished to do, or might be induced to do.

I said at the beginning of this section that opinion was not only perplexed but also divided. The division I had in mind was that between people who wanted to put pressure on the Nationalist government in order to make it change its policies and behaviour, and people who wanted to exert this pressure in order to bring that government down. Among the former there was a further division between those who were content to rely on the relatively slow effect of internal pressures, and those who were prepared to use some external levers as well. Against these gradualists were the more fervent opponents of the Nationalist régime who advocated the use of all weapons at once and as soon as possible.

The more cautious observers, influenced by motives as diverse as a genuine horror of all revolutionary activity and a desire to save existing investments, and convinced that no alternative government was possible in the immediate future, were anxious to persuade themselves and others that things were already changing for the better. They noted that householders, accustomed to a life replete with home comforts and conveniences, were beginning to feel the pinch with regard to domestic servants; they pointed to the impossibly high manufacturing costs in Bantustan; and they concluded that private citizens and industrialists would combine to force their government to modify its policies before they made life too uncomfortable or unrewarding. These meliorists were perhaps more impressed by the folly than the inhumanity of the Union government and they hoped that reasoned self-interest among the whites would produce changes which would have the consequential effect of alleviating black grievances. They were afraid that outside interference would do more harm than good by checking and negating trends already in progress.

To other observers this belief that things were already happening seemed no more than a pious hope dressed up as a diagnosis. Sceptical of the effectiveness of internal pressures, they turned their attention to external ones. The British, for example, might jolt the Natal sugar growers or the canning industry or the wine exporters. The International Bank might stop financing South African developments and force the economy back on its tracks. But was it expedient to take such action? Might it not cause the Nationalists to stiffen their necks and tighten their belts and dig in their heels? The economic weapon had certain advantages— it could be applied gradually and *sub rosa*—but so long as the prime object was to improve the behaviour of the South African government, there were always people to argue that any outside interference was more likely to exacerbate than ameliorate. The result was more argument than action.

The difference between the meliorists and the activists was that the activists aimed not to improve but to remove the Nationalist régime. They did not recoil from measures of revolutionary import. They were prepared to give encouragement to the African Congresses and to instigate trade boycotts even if the probable consequences of so doing included fresh outbreaks of violence and the collapse of the law and order (such as they were) imposed by the Nationalists. Fabian tactics seemed to them futile, for they had no faith that any significant change for the better could be engineered within the existing political framework, and so far from subscribing to the view that things were getting better they believed that things must first get worse. They regarded more Sharpevilles as inevitable and they could see no possible retort by the government except more sten guns, Saracens and death. They scouted the notion that the world's stern gaze would restrain the Nationalists from further massacres, since in their view the government had got into the position where its only choice was to kill or abdicate. The end was certain: revolution and the extinction of minority rule in South Africa as elsewhere in the continent. What was uncertain was the length of the journey before this end was reached. The best thing to do was to shorten the journey and bring on the inevitable convulsion by using every available diplomatic and economic weapon against a government which could no longer govern but only coerce and which had violated, and proposed to go on violating, legal obligations and human rights.

This line of argument was certainly more likely to lead to action than the more optimistic gradualism of the meliorists—but on one condition, namely that enough people in the right places were convinced by it. And on the whole they were not. The post-Sharpeville activists were roughly the people who had been concerned and vocal about *apartheid* before Sharpeville. One effect of Sharpeville was to attract the attention of millions who had not previously bothered themselves with South African affairs much or at all, but although this new public was roused, it was not automatically won for tough measures. The activists were again a step ahead and this was their abiding weakness. They were like expert diagnosticians whose prescriptions remained unswallowed.

Interspersed with these arguments about what should be done there was a separate argument about the effect of something which had undoubtedly happened. What was the effect of moral disapproval? The South African government was not merely isolated; it was judged and condemned. As this fact became manifest and seeped into the Union, did decent Afrikaners take note and recoil? If so, what would be the consequences for Dr. Verwoerd— or his successor? A boycott is aimed at stomachs and purses but it can also be part of a war of nerves. When Malaya stopped all trade with the Union, the gesture was economically trivial and threatened more material harm to boycotter than boycotted. But it was one among many expressions of opinion which might, when multiplied, begin to make the boycotted uneasy, for the contempt of the herd is never agreeable to any member of it, however thick his carapace. South Africa was not to be bullied or starved, but it could be and was shunned. Of course such treatment was bound to stiffen nationalist self-righteousness, while those who might respond by examining their consciences and their behaviour would be reluctant to blow the trumpets of change. And yet because man is a moral as well as a political animal, he is always vulnerable to moral shafts and even if moral disapproval works slowly—too slowly perhaps in the circumstances we have been examining— it can hardly fail to work a bit. More efficacious weapons existed but if they were not put to work, there was at least something to be said for the undermining of morale. And only a few months after Sharpeville there is an outward sign of the effect of international public opinion. As this booklet goes to press, Mr. Hammarskjöld is fully occupied with the Congo and has not yet managed to go to South Africa for the 'consultation with the Government of the Union' called for in the Security Council's resolution. But the Union government has consented to such con- sultation being held and in May Mr. Hammarskjöld was reported to have reached agreement with Mr. Louw in London on its 'character and course'. This in itself is a portent, because a few months earlier such acceptance and agreement would have seemed inconceivable.

Moreover the context of Mr. Hammarskjöld's visit has unexpectedly changed since it was first mooted. The United Nations resolution of 1 April was not much more than a piece of ritual; it witnessed more than it promised. Mr. Hammarskjöld might come and see but he could hardly conquer. He had no force behind him and his very com- petence was limited by Article 2 (7) of the Charter. South Africa was not merely able, but also entitled, to go on running its own affairs in its own unsweet way. The Charter said so—or at least it was not easy to argue to the contrary and the Secretary-General's only weapons were those of argument. But by August, things had changed, for Mr. Hammarskjöld was engaged in establishing a totally unforeseen U.N. presence in Africa and was backed not by a mere resolution of the Security Council but by the mission thrust upon him in the Congo by the fears and perplexities of statesmen of every colour, who were begin- ning to see in a U.N. authority in Africa the only chance of escaping huge affliction and dismay throughout the continent.

The Belgian Congo provides the extreme example of how not to govern a colony and in what circumstances not to leave it. The Belgians' abrupt departure, accompanied by a horrible surge of anti-white hatred, produced political disintegration, economic stagnation, violence, a collapse of elementary public services and a threat of famine. The principal world Powers were prevented by their mutual suspicions from stepping in (except to the extent of sending food); the colonial Powers were equally inhibited by their pasts and reputations; the independent African states lacked the means and resources to effect anything adequate on their own; only by using the United Nations was there any hope of restoring order and assuring a minimum living standard. The United Nations became therefore very important, the more so since the Congo's case, if extreme, is not unique. In Central Africa Nyasaland is pressing for independence and cannot much longer be put off; Northern Rhodesia will not lag far behind. Further east, in Kenya, the British have debilitated their police forces to a point where they can only keep order if nothing exceptional occurs (a most improbable contingency) and have allowed the magistracy to become so depleted that the ordinary business of assisting creditors to recover their debts is beginning to get seriously in arrears in spite of hours of overtime put in by the magistrates who remain; the credit system and therewith the economy are being jeopardised and there is a fear that people will begin taking the law into their own hands. In all these places—and the list is representative, not inclusive—law and order and regular life may break down. Perhaps only those who were in the Punjab in 1947 can appreciate to the full what such a breakdown could mean.

This intimidating situation arises out of the basic colonial dilemma: power cannot be retained indefinitely, it ought to be transferred into competent and responsible hands, these hands are too few or non-existent. The Belgians' answer was simply to drop power and clear out. The British on the other hand cling to the policy of an orderly transfer. The need for orderliness is the classic excuse for delaying but when, for other reasons, delay is no longer courted, what becomes of orderliness? The Belgians sacrificed it. The British, despite their relative successes in Ghana, Nigeria and Tanganyika, seem to be caught by the dilemma in their remaining territories. They recoil from the idea of creating a shambles by an ill-cultivated departure but they have strong reasons for leaving and have resolved to do so sooner rather than later. There is just a hope that the worst may be avoided by looking to the United Nations to provide the security and vital services which inadequately prepared African states cannot provide for themselves. So Mr. Hammarskjöld's incursion into the Congo may be no isolated episode but a prototype.

These events and portents do not dispose of Article 2 (7). The United Nations have no right to intervene except by invitation of a legally constituted government and it is not to be expected that Dr. Verwoerd[1] will ask Mr. Hammarskjöld to pull any chestnuts out of South African fires. Mr. Hammarskjöld's competence is not affected. But his standing, in the non-legal sense, is. He has become more of a man to be reckoned with in Africa, for the turn of events has led many states in many continents to wish to invest him with some of the authority which nobody else in Africa is capable of exercising in an interim period of unpredictable duration. If these states were prepared to will the means, the Secretary-General's own exceptional diplomatic talents might create something new in Africa which could touch the Union more nearly than any of the threats uttered or actions proposed in the first months after Sharpeville. Mr. Hammarskjöld would go to Pretoria as something, if indefinably, more than a suppliant or an explorer.

[1] Or Sir Edgar Whitehead, who provoked a minor Sharpeville at the end of July by injudicious arrests of moderate African leaders and thus put an end to Southern Rhodesia's boast to have managed its affairs for sixty-four years without any deaths of this kind.

Still Mr. Hammarskjöld is not an independent power. He operates on instructions given him by independent powers (if they can agree), and paradoxically the significance of his emergence as a leading actor on the international stage lies precisely in the fact that he is not automotive; that he does no more than provide automotive powers with a means for doing things which they would not care to do severally and in their own name. States, like individuals, sometimes wish to take certain steps but on weighing the consequences hesitate and remain inert. If they can see a way of achieving their purpose without taking the feared steps, they might discard their inertia on the principle that there are some things which can be done through an agent but not otherwise. If moreover there were a legal case for action, the hesitant might find themselves hesitating to abstain instead of hesitating to co-operate. Hence the importance of the South West African mandate. On the issue of *apartheid* some governments would incline to observe the formal injunction of Article 2 (7), which bade them hold to the basic tenets of state sovereignty and not interfere in another state's internal affairs, but if the International Court were to rule in contentious proceedings that the mandate agreement had been broken, the inclination would be the other way: the fortunes or misfortunes of a mandated territory are not the internal affair of the mandatory and many states would find it embarrassing to go on ignoring the findings of so respected a body as the Court. They might then be willing to associate themselves with a combined operation to be conducted in the name of the United Nations and under the general direction of Mr. Hammarskjöld. Economic sanctions on a convincing scale could even be envisaged, directed essentially against South Africa's internal policies but set in motion as a result of two external factors which neither world opinion nor sovereign governments could ignore: the threats to peace exemplified in the Congo and the defiance of international agreements perpetrated in South West Africa.

APPENDIXES

I. SPEECH BY MR. HAROLD MACMILLAN TO THE SOUTH AFRICAN PARLIAMENT, CAPE TOWN, 3 FEBRUARY 1960

IT is a great privilege to be invited to address members of both Houses of the Union Parliament. It is a unique privilege to do so in 1960, just half a century after the Parliament of the Union came to birth. I am especially grateful to your Prime Minister, Dr. Verwoerd, who invited me to visit your country and arranged for me to address you here today.

It is fitting that my tour of Africa should culminate in the Union parliament in the town so long Europe's gateway to the Indian Ocean and the East. I am most grateful to your government for all the trouble they have taken in making the arrangements, which have enabled me to see so much in so short a time. Wherever we have gone in town or in country, we have been received in a spirit of friendship and affection which has warmed our hearts, and we value this the more because we know that it is an expression of your good will, not only to ourselves but to all the people of Britain.

It is, as I have said, a special privilege for me to be here in 1960, when you are celebrating the golden wedding of the Union. At such a time it is natural and right that you should pause to take stock of your position—to look back at what you have achieved and to look forward to what lies ahead.

In the fifty years of their nationhood the people of South Africa have built a strong economy founded on healthy agriculture and thriving and resilient industries.

During my visit I have been able to see something of your mining industry, on which the prosperity of your country is so firmly based. I have seen your Iron and Steel Corporation, and visited your Council for Scientific and Industrial Research at Pretoria. These two bodies, in their different ways, are symbols of a lively forward-looking and expanding economy.

I have seen the great city of Durban, with its wonderful port, and the skyscrapers of Johannesburg standing where seventy years ago there was nothing but open veldt. I have seen, too, the fine cities of Pretoria and Bloemfontein.

No one could fail to be impressed by the immense material progress which has been achieved. That all this has been accomplished in so short a time is a striking testimony to the initiative, energy, and skill of your people.

We in Britain are proud of the contribution we have made to this remarkable achievement. Much of it has been financed by British capital. According to a recent survey made by the Union government, nearly two-thirds of oversea investment outstanding in the Union at the end of 1956 was British.

But that is not all. We have developed trade between us to our common advantage, and our economies are now largely interdependent. You export to us raw materials and food—and, of course, gold—and we in return send you consumer goods and capital equipment. We take a third of all your exports and we supply a third of all your imports.

This broad traditional pattern of investment and trade has been maintained in spite of changes brought about by the development of our two economies. It gives me great encouragement to reflect that the economies of both our countries, while developing rapidly have yet remained interdependent and capable of sustaining one another. Britain has always been your best customer and, as your new industries develop, we believe we can be your best partners, too.

In addition to building this strong economy within your own borders, you have also played your part as an independent nation in world affairs. As a soldier in the First World War, and as a Minister in Sir Winston Churchill's government in the Second, I know personally the value of the contribution which your forces made to victory in the cause of freedom. I know something, too, of the inspiration which General Smuts brought to us in Britain in our darkest hours. Again, in the Korean crisis, you played your full part.

Thus, in testing times of war and aggression, your statesmen and your soldiers have made their influence felt far beyond the African continent. In the period of reconstruction, when Dr. Malan was your Prime Minister, your resources greatly assisted the recovery of the sterling area in the post-war world.

Now, in the no less difficult task of peace, your leaders in industry, commerce, and finance continue to be prominent in world affairs.

Today, your readiness to provide technical assistance to the less well-developed parts of Africa is of immense help to the countries which receive it. It is also a source of strength to your friends in the Commonwealth and elsewhere in the western world.

You are collaborating in the work of the Commission for Technical Cooperation in Africa South of the Sahara, and now in the United Nations Economic Commission for Africa. Your Minister of External Affairs intends to visit Ghana later this year. All this proves your determination, as the most advanced industrial country of the continent, to play your part in the new Africa of today.

As I have travelled through the Union I have found everywhere, as I expected, a deep preoccupation with what is happening in the rest of the African continent. I understand and sympathise with your interest in these events, and your anxiety about them.

Ever since the break-up of the Roman Empire one of the constant facts of political life in Europe has been the emergence of independent nations. They have come into existence over the centuries in different shapes with different forms of government. But all have been inspired with a keen feeling of nationalism, which has grown as nations have grown.

In the twentieth century, and especially since the end of the war, the processes which gave birth to the nation-states of Europe have been repeated all over the world. We have seen the awakening of national consciousness in peoples who have for centuries lived in dependence on some other power.

Fifteen years ago this movement spread through Asia. Many countries there, of different races and civilisations, pressed their claim to an independent national life.

Today, the same thing is happening in Africa. The most striking of all the impressions I have formed since I left London a month ago is of the strength of this African national consciousness. In different places it may take different forms, but it is happening everywhere. The wind of change is blowing through the continent.

Whether we like it or not, this growth of national consciousness is a political fact. We must all accept it as a fact. Our national policies must take account of it.

Of course, you understand this as well as anyone. You are sprung from Europe, the home of nationalism. And here in Africa you have yourselves created a full nation— a new nation. Indeed, in the history of our times yours will be recorded as the first of the African nationalisms.

And this tide of national consciousness which is now rising in Africa is a fact for which you and we and the other nations of the western world are ultimately responsible.

For its causes are to be found in the achievements of western civilisation in pushing forward the frontiers of knowledge, applying science in the service of human needs, expanding food production, speeding and multiplying means of communication, and, above all, spreading education.

As I have said, the growth of national consciousness in Africa is a political fact and we must accept it as such. I sincerely believe that if we cannot do so, we may imperil the precarious balance of east and west on which the peace of the world depends.

The world today is divided into three great groups. First, there are what we call the western Powers. You in South Africa and we in Britain belong to this group, together with our friends and allies in other parts of the Commonwealth, in the United States of America, and in Europe.

Secondly, there are the communists—Russia and her satellites in Europe and China, whose population will rise by 1970 to the staggering total of 800 million. Thirdly, there are those parts of the world whose people are at present uncommitted either to communism or to our western ideas. In this context we think first of Asia and of Africa.

As I see it, the great issue in this second half of the twentieth century is whether the uncommitted peoples of Asia and Africa will swing to the east or to the west. Will they be drawn into the communist camp? Or will the great experiments in self-government that are now being made in Asia and Africa, especially within the Commonwealth, prove so successful, and by their example so compelling, that the balance will come down in favour of freedom and order and justice?

The struggle is joined and it is a struggle for the minds of men. What is now on trial is much more than our military strength or our diplomatic and administrative skill. It is our way of life.

The uncommitted nations want to see before they choose. What can we show them to help them choose aright? Each of the independent members of the Commonwealth must answer that question for itself.

It is the basic principle for our modern Commonwealth that we respect each other's sovereignty in matters of internal policy. At the same time, we must recognise that, in this shrinking world in which we live today, the internal policies of one nation may have effects outside it. We may sometimes be tempted to say to each other, 'Mind your own business.' But in these days I would myself expand the old saying so that it runs, 'Mind your own business, but mind how it affects my business, too.'

Let me be very frank with you, my friends. What governments and parliaments in the United Kingdom have done since the war in according independence to India, Pakistan, Ceylon, Malaya, and Ghana, and what they will do for Nigeria and the other countries now nearing independence—all this, though we take full and sole responsibility for it, we do in the belief that it is the only way to establish the future of the Commonwealth and of the free world on sound foundations.

All this, of course, is also of deep and close concern to you, for nothing we do in this small world can be done in a corner or remain hidden. What we do today in West, Central, and East Africa becomes known to everyone in the Union, whatever his language, colour, or tradition.

Let me assure you in all friendliness that we are well aware of this, and that we have acted and will act with full knowledge of the responsibility we have to you and to all our friends. Nevertheless, I am sure you will agree that in our own areas of responsibility we must each do what we think right. What we think right derives from long experience, both of failure and success in the management of our own affairs.

We have tried to learn and apply the lessons of both. Our judgment of right and wrong and of justice is rooted in the same soil as yours—in Christianity and in the rule of law as the basis of a free society.

This experience of our own explains why it has been our aim, in countries for which we have borne responsibility, not only to raise the material standards of living but to create a society which respects the rights of individuals—a society in which men are given the opportunity to grow to their full stature, and that must in our view include the opportunity to have an increasing share in political power and responsibility; a society in which individual merit, and individual merit alone, is the criterion for man's advancement whether political or economic.

Finally, in countries inhabited by several different

races, it has been our aim to find the means by which the community can become more of a community, and fellowship can be fostered between its various parts.

This problem is by no means confined to Africa, nor is it always the problem of the European minority. In Malaya, for instance, though there are Indian and European minorities, Malays and Chinese make up the great bulk of the population, and the Chinese are not much fewer in numbers than Malays. Yet these two peoples must learn to live together in harmony and unity, and the strength of Malaya as a nation will depend on the different contributions which the two races can make.

The attitude of the United Kingdom government towards this problem was clearly expressed by the Foreign Secretary, Mr. Selwyn Lloyd, speaking at the United Nations General Assembly on 17 September 1959. These are his words:

'In those territories where different races or tribes live side by side, the task is to ensure that all the people may enjoy security and freedom and the chance to contribute as individuals to the progress and well being of these countries. We reject the idea of any inherent superiority of one race over another. Our policy therefore is non-racial. It offers a future in which Africans, Europeans, Asians, the peoples of the Pacific, and others with whom we are concerned, will all play their full part as citizens in the countries where they live and in which feelings of race will be submerged in loyalty to the new nations.'

I have thought you would wish me to state plainly and with full candour the policy for which we in Britain stand.

It may well be that in trying to do our duty as we see it, we shall sometimes make difficulties for you. If this proves to be so, we shall regret it.

But I know that even so, you would not ask us to flinch from doing our duty. You, too, will do your duty as you see it.

I am well aware of the peculiar nature of the problems

with which you are faced here in the Union of South
Africa. I know the differences between your situation and
that of most of the other states in Africa.

You have here some three million people of European
origin. This country is their home. It has been their home
for many generations. They have no other. The same is
true of the Europeans in Central and East Africa.

In most other African states, those who have come from
Europe have come to work, to contribute their skills, perhaps to teach, but not to make a home.

The problems to which you members of the Union
parliament have to address yourselves are very different
from those which face the parliaments of countries with
homogeneous populations. These are complicated and
baffling problems. It would be surprising if your interpretation of your duty did not sometimes produce very
different results from ours in terms of government policies
and actions.

As a fellow member of the Commonwealth, it is our
earnest desire to give South Africa our support and encouragement, but I hope you won't mind my saying
frankly that there are some aspects of your policies which
make it impossible for us to do this without being false to
our own deep convictions about the political destinies of
free men, to which in our own territories we are trying to
give effect.

I think we ought as friends to face together—without
seeking to apportion credit or blame—the fact that in the
world of today this difference of outlook lies between us.

I said that I was speaking as a friend. I can also claim
to be speaking as a relation. For we Scots can claim family
connexions with both great European sections of your
population, not only with the English-speaking people
but with Afrikaans-speaking as well.

This is a point which hardly needs emphasis in Cape
Town, where you can see every day the statue of that great
Scotsman, Andrew Murray. His work in the Dutch

Reformed Church in the Cape, and the work of his son in the Orange Free State, was among Afrikaans-speaking people. There has always been a very close connexion between the Church of Scotland and the Church of the Netherlands. The Synod of Dort plays the same great part in the history of both. Many aspirants to the Ministry of Scotland, especially in the seventeenth and eighteenth centuries, went to pursue their theological studies in the Netherlands. Scotland can claim to have repaid the debt in South Africa. I am thinking particularly of the Scots in the Orange Free State. Not only the younger Andrew Murray, but also the Robertsons, the Frasers, the McDonalds—families which have been called the Free State clans who became burghers of the old Free State and whose descendants still play their part there.

But though I count myself a Scot, my mother was American, and the United States provides a valuable illustration of one of the main points which I have been trying to make in my remarks today. Its population, like yours, is a blend of many different strains, and over the years most of those who have gone to North America have gone there in order to escape conditions in Europe which they found intolerable.

It is not surprising, therefore, that for so many years a main objective of American statesmen, supported by the American public, was to isolate themselves from Europe, and with their great material strength and vast resources open to them this might have seemed an attractive and practicable course.

Nevertheless, in the two world wars of this century, they have found themselves unable to stand aside. Twice their manpower in arms has streamed back across the Atlantic to shed its blood in those European struggles from which their ancestors thought they would escape by emigrating to the new world. And when the second war was over, they were forced to recognise that in the small world of today isolationism is out of date and offers no assurance of security.

The fact is that in this modern world no country, not even the greatest, can live for itself alone. It has always been impossible for individual man to live in isolation from his fellows—in home, tribe, village, or city. Today it is impossible for nations to live in isolation from one another. All nations are interdependent, one upon another, and this is generally realised throughout the western world. I hope in due course the countries of communism will recognise it too.

It was certainly with that thought in mind that I took the decision to visit Moscow about this time last year. Russia has been isolationist in her time and still has tendencies that way, but the fact remains that we must live in the same world with Russia and we must find a way of doing so. I believe that the initiative which we took last year has had some success, although grave difficulties may arise. Nevertheless I think nothing but good can come out of extending contacts between individuals, contacts in trade and from the exchange of visitors.

The members of the Commonwealth feel particularly strongly the value of interdependence. They are as independent as any countries in the shrinking world can be, but they have voluntarily agreed to work together. I certainly do not believe in refusing to trade with people just because you dislike the way they manage their internal affairs at home. Boycotts will never get you anywhere.

Here I would like to say in parenthesis that I deprecate attempts which are being made in Britain today to organise a consumer boycott of South African goods. It has never been the practice of any government in the United Kingdom, including a Labour government, to undertake or support campaigns of this kind designed to influence the internal policies of another Commonwealth country.

They recognise that there may be differences between them in their institutions or in their internal policies, and membership does not imply either a wish to express a judgment on these matters or a need to impose a stifling uniformity.

It is, I think, a help that there has never been a question of any rigid constitution for the Commonwealth. Perhaps this is because we have got on well enough in the United Kingdom without a written constitution and tend to look suspiciously at them.

Whether that is so or not, it is quite clear that a rigid constitutional framework for the Commonwealth would not work. At the first of the stresses and strains which are inevitable in this period of history, cracks would appear in the framework and the whole structure would crumble. It is the flexibility of our Commonwealth institutions which gives them their strength.

In conclusion, may I say this. I have spoken frankly about the differences between our two countries in their approach to one of the great current problems with which each has to deal within its own sphere of responsibility. These differences are well known, they are matters of public knowledge—indeed, of public controversy. And I should have been less than honest if, by remaining silent on them, I had seemed to imply that they did not exist.

But differences on one subject, important though it is, need not and should not impair our capacity to co-operate with one another in furthering the many practical interests which we share in common. The independent members of the Commonwealth do not always agree on every subject. It is not a condition of their association that they should do so. On the contrary, the strength of our Commonwealth lies largely in the fact that it is a free association of in-dependent sovereign States, each responsible for ordering its own affairs but co-operating in the pursuit of common aims and purposes in world affairs.

Moreover, these differences may be transitory. In time, they may be resolved. Our duty is to see them in perspective against the background of our long association.

Of this, at any rate, I am certain. Those of us who, by the grace of the electorate, are temporarily in charge of affairs in my country and in yours have no right to sweep aside on this account the friendship that exists between our two countries. For that is the legacy of history. It is not ours alone to deal with as we wish.

We must face the differences. But let us try to see beyond them down the long vista of the future. I hope—indeed I am confident—that in another fifty years we shall look back on the differences that exist between us now as matters of historical interest.

For as time passes and one generation yields to another, human problems change and fade. Let us remember these truths. Let us resolve to build, not to destroy. And let us remember always that weakness comes from division, and strength from unity.—*Reuter*.

II. STATEMENT ISSUED BY THE DEPARTMENT OF STATE, WASHINGTON, 22 MARCH 1960

The United States deplores violence in all its forms and hopes the African people of South Africa will be able to obtain redress for legitimate grievances by peaceful means. While the United States as a matter of practice does not ordinarily comment on the internal affairs of governments with which it enjoys normal relations, it cannot help but regret the tragic loss of life resulting from the measures taken against the demonstrators in South Africa.

III. EXTRACTS FROM THE COMMUNIQUÉ OF THE COMMONWEALTH PRIME MINISTERS' CONFERENCE, LONDON, 13 MAY 1960

The Meeting noted a statement by the South African Minister of External Affairs that the Union government intended to hold a referendum on the subject of South Africa becoming a republic. The meeting affirmed the view that the choice between a monarchy and a republic was entirely the responsibility of the country concerned. In the event of South Africa deciding to become a republic

and if the desire was subsequently expressed to remain a
member of the Commonwealth, the Meeting suggested
that the South African government should then ask for
the consent of the other Commonwealth governments
either at a Meeting of Commonwealth Prime Ministers, or,

. . . .

if this were not practicable, by correspondence . . .

. . . Whilst reaffirming the traditional practice that Commonwealth conferences do not discuss the internal affairs
of member countries Ministers availed themselves of
Mr. Louw's presence in London to have informal discussions with him about the racial situation in South
Africa. During these informal discussions Mr. Louw gave
information and answered questions on the Union's
policies, and the other Ministers conveyed to him their
views on the South African problem. The Ministers
emphasised that the Commonwealth itself is a multi-racial
association and expressed the need to ensure good relations
between all member states and peoples of the Commonwealth.

IV. ARTICLES 2 (7), 55 AND 56 OF THE CHARTER OF THE UNITED NATIONS

Article 2 (7)

Nothing contained in the present Charter shall authorise
the United Nations to intervene in matters which are
essentially within the domestic jurisdiction of any state or
shall require the Members to submit such matters to
settlement under the present Charter; but this principle
shall not prejudice the application of enforcement measures
under Chapter VII. (Chapter VII deals with 'action with
respect to threats to the peace, breaches of the peace and
acts of aggression'.)

Article 55

With a view to the creation of conditions of stability
and well-being which are necessary for peaceful and friendly

relations among nations based on respect for the principle of equal rights and self-determination of peoples, the United Nations shall promote:

a. higher standards of living, full employment, and conditions of economic and social progress and development;

b. solutions of international economic, social, health, and related problems; and international cultural and educational co-operation; and

c. universal respect for, and observance of, human rights and fundamental freedoms for all without distinction as to race, sex, language, or religion.

Article 56

All members pledge themselves to take joint and separate action in co-operation with the Organisation for the achievement of the purposes set forth in Article 55.

V. RESOLUTION OF THE SECURITY COUNCIL, 1 APRIL 1960

The Security Council,

Having considered the complaint of twenty-nine Member States contained in document S/4279 and Add. 1 concerning 'the situation arising out of the large-scale killings of unarmed and peaceful demonstrators against racial discrimination and segregation in the Union of South Africa',

Recognising that such a situation has been brought about by the racial policies of the Government of the Union of South Africa and the continued disregard by that government of the resolutions of the General Assembly calling upon it to revise its policies and bring them into conformity with its obligations and responsibilities under the Charter,

Taking into account the strong feelings and grave concern

aroused among governments and peoples of the world by the happenings in the Union of South Africa,

1. *Recognises* that the situation in the Union of South Africa is one that has led to international friction and if continued might endanger international peace and security;

2. *Deplores* that the recent disturbances in the Union of South Africa should have led to the loss of life of so many Africans and extends to the families of the victims its deepest sympathies;

3. *Deplores* the policies and actions of the Government of the Union of South Africa which have given rise to the present situation;

4. *Calls upon* the Government of the Union of South Africa to initiate measures aimed at bringing about racial harmony based on equality, in order to ensure that the present situation does not continue or recur and to abandon its policies of apartheid and racial discrimination;

5. *Requests* the Secretary-General, in consultation with the Government of the Union of South Africa, to make such arrangements as would adequately help in upholding the purposes and principles of the Charter and to report to the Security Council whenever necessary and appropriate.

VI. ARTICLE 22 OF THE COVENANT OF THE LEAGUE OF NATIONS

1. To those colonies and territories which as a consequence of the late war have ceased to be under the sovereignty of the States which formerly governed them and which are inhabited by peoples not yet able to stand by themselves under the strenuous conditions of the modern world, there should be applied the principle that the well-being and the development of such peoples form a sacred trust of civilisation and that securities for the performance of this trust should be embodied in this Covenant.

2. The best method of giving practical effect to this principle is that the tutelage of such peoples should be intrusted to advanced nations who by reason of their resources, their experience or their geographical position can best undertake this responsibility, and who are willing to accept it, and that this tutelage should be exercised by them as Mandatories on behalf of the League.

3. The character of the mandate must differ according to the stage of the development of the people, the geographical position of the territory, its economic conditions and other similar circumstances.

4. Certain communities formerly belonging to the Turkish Empire have reached a stage of development where their existence as independent nations can be provisionally recognised subject to the rendering of administrative advice and assistance by a Mandatory until such time as they are able to stand alone. The wishes of these communities must be a principal consideration in the selection of the Mandatory.

5. Other peoples, especially those of Central Africa, are at such a stage that the Mandatory must be responsible for the administration of the territory under conditions which will guarantee freedom of conscience and religion, subject only to the maintenance of public order and morals, the prohibition of abuses such as the slave trade, the arms traffic and the liquor traffic, and the prevention of the establishment of fortifications of military and naval bases and of military training of the natives for other than police purposes and the defense of territory, and will also secure equal opportunities for the trade and commerce of other Members of the League.

6. There are territories, such as South West Africa and certain of the South Pacific islands, which, owing to the sparseness of their population, or their small size, or their remoteness from the centers of civilisation, or their geographical contiguity to the territory of the Mandatory, and other circumstances, can be best administered under

the laws of the Mandatory as integral portions of its territory, subject to the safeguards above mentioned in the interests of the indigenous population.

7. In every case of mandate, the Mandatory shall render to the Council an annual report in reference to the territory committed to its charge.

8. The degree of authority, control or administration to be exercised by the Mandatory shall, if not previously agreed upon by the Members of the League, be explicitly defined in each case by the Council.

9. A permanent Commission shall be constituted to receive and examine the annual reports of the Mandatories and to advise the Council on all matters relating to the observance of the Mandates.

VII. AGREEMENT CONCERNING THE MANDATE OVER SOUTH WEST AFRICA, 17 DECEMBER, 1920

THE COUNCIL OF THE LEAGUE OF NATIONS:

Whereas by Article 119 of the Treaty of Peace with Germany signed at Versailles on June 28 1919, Germany renounced in favour of the Principal Allied and Associated Powers all her rights over her oversea possessions, including therein German South West Africa; and

Whereas the Principal Allied and Associated Powers agreed that, in accordance with Article 22, Part I (Covenant of the League of Nations) of the said Treaty, a Mandate should be conferred upon His Britannic Majesty to be exercised on his behalf by the Government of the Union of South Africa to administer the territory aforementioned, and have proposed that the Mandate should be formulated on the following terms; and

Whereas His Britannic Majesty, for and on behalf of the Government of the Union of South Africa, has agreed to accept the Mandate in respect of the said territory and has undertaken to exercise it on behalf of the League of Nations in accordance with the following provisions; and

Whereas, by the afore-mentioned Article 22, paragraph 8, it is provided that the degree of authority, control or administration to be exercised by the Mandatory not having been previously agreed upon by the Members of the League, shall be explicitly defined by the Council of the League of Nations:

Confirming the said Mandate, defines its terms as follows:

Article 1

The territory over which a Mandate is conferred upon His Britannic Majesty for and on behalf of the Government of the Union of South Africa (hereinafter called the Mandatory) comprises the territory which formerly constituted the German Protectorate of South West Africa.

Article 2

The Mandatory shall have full power of administration and legislation over the territory subject to the present Mandate as an integral portion of the Union of South Africa, and may apply the laws of the Union of South Africa to the territory, subject to such local modifications as circumstances may require.

The Mandatory shall promote to the utmost the material and moral well-being and the social progress of the inhabitants of the territory subject to the present Mandate.

Article 3

The Mandatory shall see that the slave trade is prohibited, and that no forced labour is permitted, except for essential public works and services, and then only for adequate remuneration.

The Mandatory shall also see that the traffic in arms and ammunition is controlled in accordance with principles analogous to those laid down in the Convention relating to the control of the arms traffic, signed on September 10, 1919, or in any convention amending the same.

The supply of intoxicating spirits and beverages to the natives shall be prohibited.

Article 4

The military training of the natives, otherwise than for purposes of internal police and the local defence of the territory, shall be prohibited. Furthermore, no military or naval bases shall be established or fortifications erected in the territory.

Article 5

Subject to the provisions of any local law for the maintenance of public order and public morals, the Mandatory shall ensure in the territory freedom of conscience and the free exercise of all forms of worship, and shall allow all missionaries, nationals of any State Member of the League of Nations, to enter into, travel and reside in the territory for the purpose of prosecuting their calling.

Article 6

The Mandatory shall make to the Council of the League of Nations an annual report to the satisfaction of the Council, containing full information with regard to the territory, and indicating the measures taken to carry out the obligations assumed under Articles 2, 3, 4 and 5.

Article 7

The consent of the Council of the League of Nations is required for any modification of the terms of the present Mandate. The Mandatory agrees that, if any dispute whatever should arise between the Mandatory and another Member of the League of Nations relating to the interpretation or the application of the provisions of the Mandate such dispute, if it cannot be settled by negotiation, shall be submitted to the Permanent Court of International Justice provided for by Article 14 of the Covenant of the League of Nations.

The present Declaration shall be deposited in the archives of the League of Nations. Certified copies shall be forwarded by the Secretary-General of the League of Nations to all Powers Signatories of the Treaty of Peace with Germany.

Certified true copy
Secretary-General

Made at Geneva the 17th day of December, 1920.

VIII. RESOLUTIONS OF THE CONFERENCE OF INDEPENDENT AFRICAN STATES, ADDIS ABABA, 14–26 JUNE 1960

1. *On South West Africa*

'The Conference of Independent African States meeting at Addis Ababa,

A. **Having considered** the question of the Territory of South West Africa;

B. **Recalling** United Nations Resolution 1361 (XIV) of November 17 1959 which drew "the attention of Member States to the conclusions of the special report of the Committee on South West Africa covering the legal action open to Member States to refer any dispute with the Union of South Africa concerning the interpretation or application of the Mandate for South West Africa to the International Court of Justice for adjudication in accordance with Article 37 of the Statute of the Court";

(i) **Concludes** that the international obligations of the Union of South Africa concerning the Territory of South West Africa should be submitted to the International Court of Justice for adjudication in a contentious proceeding;

(ii) **Notes** that the Governments of Ethiopia and of Liberia have signified their intention to institute such a proceeding;

(iii) **Decides** that a Steering Committee of four African States including the delegations of Ethiopia and of Liberia, should be established to determine the procedures and tactics incident to the conduct of the juridical proceedings in this matter.'

2. *On Economic Measures Against South Africa*
'The Conference of Independent African States meeting in Addis Ababa,

Having learned with indignation of the death of many African political leaders in the prisons of the Union of South Africa thus adding to the already long list of victims of the shameful policy of racial discrimination;

Recalling Resolution No. 1375 (XIV) adopted by the United Nations General Assembly condemning the policy of apartheid and racial discrimination practised by the Government of the Union of South Africa;

Recalling further the Security Council's Resolution of April 1 1960 recognising the existence of a situation in South Africa which, if continued, might endanger international peace and security;

Reaffirming the declaration of Bandung and the resolutions adopted at Accra and Monrovia regarding this shameful policy;

Noting that, despite world opinion and the resolutions adopted by the United Nations, the Government of the Union of South Africa still persists in its evil policy of apartheid and racial discrimination;

(i) **Desires** to pay homage to all victims of the shameful policy of apartheid and racial discrimination;

(ii) **Decides** to assist the victims of racial discrimination and furnish them with all the means necessary to attain their political objectives of liberty and democracy;

(iii) **Calls** upon member states to sever diplomatic relations or refrain from establishing diplomatic relations as the case may be, to close African ports to all vessels flying the South African flag, to enact legislation prohibiting their ships from entering South African ports, to boycott all South African goods, to refuse landing and passage facilities to all aircraft belonging to the government and companies registered under the laws of the Union of South Africa, and to prohibit all South African aircraft from flying over the air space of the Independent African States;

(iv) **Invites** the Arab States to approach all petroleum companies with a view to preventing Arab oil from being sold to the Union of South Africa and recommends that the African States refuse any concession to any company which continues to sell petroleum to the Union of South Africa;

(v) **Invites** the Independent African States which are members of the British Commonwealth to take all possible steps to secure the exclusion of the Union of South Africa from the British Commonwealth;

(vi) **Recommends** that appropriate measures be taken by the United Nations in accordance with Article 41 of the Charter;

(vii) **Appeals** to world public opinion to persevere in the effort to put an end to the terrible situation caused by apartheid and racial discrimination;

(viii) **Decides** to instruct the Informal Permanent Machinery to take all steps necessary to secure that effect shall be given to the above recommendations and to furnish full information on cases of racial discrimination in the Union of South Africa so that the outside world may be correctly informed about such practices.'

IX. SOME STATISTICS

1. South African imports of petroleum and related products 1956–9.

(Percentages)

	1956	1957	1958	1959
Iran	28	59	75	69
Saudi Arabia	42	14	5	7
Bahrein	15	14	11	7
Aden	9	9	2	3
Total Middle East	94	96	93	86
Indonesia	2	3	4	3
Others	4	1	3	11
	100	100	100	100

2. Direction of South African imports and exports 1956–9.[1]

(£ millions)

Imports	UK	USA	Federal Germany	Canada	Japan	Netherlands	Central African Federation	Total
1956	157	99	32	23	12	10	18	495
1957	179	108	44	17	18	11	14	550
1958	187	97	58	18	15	11	12	555
1959	152	83	50	19	15	12	12	489
% in 1959	31	17	10	5	4	2	2	71

Exports	UK	Central African Federation	USA	Belgium	Federal Germany	France	Italy	Total
1956	108	55	29	21	18	15	17	366
1957	110	58	25	18	20	15	17	397
1958	107	49	25	14	14	11	15	357
1959	110	53	35	17	16	13	13	389
% in 1959	28	14	9	4	4	3	3	65

[1] Figures taken from South African Government Yearbooks.

3. Categories of South African imports 1950 and 1955–7, and exports, 1936/7 and 1954/5–56/7.[1]

Imports

	1950	1955	1956	1957
		(Percentages)		
Metals and manufactures (including machinery and vehicles)	32·6	37·5	43·8	45·4
Fibres, yarns, textiles and apparel	22·1	18·5	17·2	17·6
Mineral and vegetable oils, waxes and paints	10·9	9·8	10·4	10·1
Food, beverages and tobacco	6·9	5·4	5·4	4·1
Drugs, chemicals and fertilisers	3·1	4·3	4·1	4·0

Exports

	1936/7	1954/5	1955/6	1956/7
Gold	69·7	35·1	35·4	33·3
Animal and vegetable products	20·1	25·2	22·8	24·7
Minerals and metals	7·0	20·3	22·6	24·0
Manufactured goods	3·2	19·4	19·0	18·0

[1] Taken from *Economic Survey of Africa since 1950*, pp. 165 and 171

Printed in Great Britain by R. J. Acford, Ltd.,
Industrial Estate, Chichester, Sussex.

Date Due

JUN 21 1979		
FEB 28 1980		
MAR 19 1981		
APR 5 1984		
MAY 24 1984		
NOV 20 1986		
DEC 11 1986		
DEC 18 1987		
OCT 24 1988		